MAD for ADS

How Advertising Gets (and Stays) in Our Heads

Written by
Erica Fyvie

Illustrated by
Ian Turner

Kids Can Press

This book is dedicated to Jay, Liv and Grace, with love and gratitude — E.F.
To Gordie and Ida — I.T.

Text © 2021 Erica Fyvie
Illustrations © 2021 Ian Turner

Published in Canada and the U.S. by Kids Can Press Ltd.
25 Dockside Drive, Toronto, ON M5A 0B5

Kids Can Press is a Corus Entertainment Inc. company

www.kidscanpress.com

The artwork in this book was rendered digitally.
The text is set in Colby.

Edited by Jennifer Stokes and Kathleen Keenan
Designed by Barb Kelly

Printed and bound in Shenzhen, China, in 10/2020 by C & C Offset

CM 21 0 9 8 7 6 5 4 3 2 1

Library and Archives Canada Cataloguing in Publication

Title: Mad for ads : how advertising gets (and stays) in our heads / written by Erica Fyvie ; illustrated by Ian Turner.

Names: Fyvie, Erica, 1973– author. | Turner, Ian (Ian J.), illustrator.

Description: Includes bibliographical references and index.

Identifiers: Canadiana 20200237845 | ISBN 9781525301315 (hardcover)

Subjects: LCSH: Advertising — Juvenile literature. | LCSH: Advertising — Psychological aspects — Juvenile literature.

Classification: LCC HF5829 .F98 2021 | DDC j659.1 — dc23

Kids Can Press gratefully acknowledges that the land on which our office is located is the traditional territory of many nations, including the Mississaugas of the Credit, the Anishnabeg, the Chippewa, the Haudenosaunee and the Wendat peoples, and is now home to many diverse First Nations, Inuit and Métis peoples.

We thank the Government of Ontario, through Ontario Creates; the Ontario Arts Council; the Canada Council for the Arts; and the Government of Canada for supporting our publishing activity.

CONTENTS

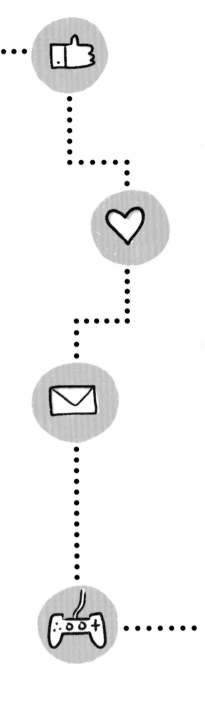

INTRODUCTION   4

Chapter ONE:
A *Brand* New AD-venture   6

Chapter TWO:
An AD-venture into Promotion   12

Chapter THREE:
Map This AD-venture   20

Chapter FOUR:
An AD-venture into Your Brain on Ads   32

Chapter FIVE:
An AD-venture Tracker   44

Chapter SIX:
A Time Travel AD-venture   52

Chapter SEVEN:
An AD-venture into Your Personal Brand   54

CONCLUSION   58

Glossary   60

Bibliography   62

Index   63

INTRODUCTION

The messages of advertising hit you all the time, from all angles and at every stage of your life. Ads can make you laugh. They can make you cry. Some ads are so surprising they stop you in your tracks. Your parents may find certain ads unacceptable because they promote something they don't want you to have. You might appreciate those same ads for their creativity and striking visuals.

An ad can be confusing if you're not sure what it's selling. A product? A lifestyle?

An ad can be inspiring if it makes you feel connected to something bigger.

The purpose of this book is to help you understand the business of advertising. It's a highly creative one. It's also highly complex — targeting a full range of your emotions. With visuals everywhere you look, advertising may seem like an external thing. But *this* AD-venture is interested in how ads affect your internal world: your thoughts, your feelings and your sense of self.

Get your passport ready! Let's go out into this advertised world and see how the AD-venture begins …

Representation Matters

How many commercials do you see that feature someone with a disability in a lead role? In advertising, some of us are heard; others, not so much. Advertising that features people of color and gender diversity is becoming more mainstream, mostly because equal rights advocates have been fighting behind the scenes for decades. **Representation** matters. Advertising is a more interesting industry when more lives are validated as important consumers. If we don't see ourselves in the media mirror, what does that mean about the worth of our stories?

Chapter ONE

A *Brand* New AD-venture

Let's dress for this AD-venture.

What are you wearing right now? Hand-me-downs? Clothes that were a gift? Thrift store finds? Or an outfit from a giant retail store?

What do you like about what you're wearing? Do you feel good in it? Do your clothes reflect your sense of style? Do you just like to be comfortable? Maybe it was simply the first thing you found on your bedroom floor!

Now, let's go beyond what you're wearing. What's the last thing you posted online? What was the last food or drink you bought? What song do you play on repeat?

All of these decisions reflect a combination of your own beliefs, wishes, style and taste. Here's another way of putting it: you have created your own brand — and that brand is *you*. The way you step out into the world is your brand. This means you probably already understand something about the way advertising works.

The brands you support — what you wear, eat, watch, buy, keep ... everything! — communicate something about you.

You also contribute to your brand through social media. What you post, share and like online create a personality. For example, you might be thinking of a certain person or group of people when you post something — that's your **target audience**. And maybe you only post photos where you're surrounded by friends — which might mean you brand yourself as "popular."

Some social media users are well aware of their analytics and closely monitor the number of likes and followers they get from each post. This kind of background data was once only a corporate tool, but now we can all use it to assess the value of our very own online brands.

What are the brands that contribute to *your* brand?

3000 Messages

Creating a brand personality takes time. Some of the products we use today have been around for decades, some for over 100 years, and they might have an instantly recognizable logo or image. (You can probably think of a few of these.)

How are these corporate brands being built? Studies tell us that we see *3000 advertised messages every day*. If someone said 3000 things to you in another language every day, wouldn't you try to understand what they're saying? If *one* person said something to you, it can be tuned out. But if *3000* people did? Sheesh, that's a lot of noise!

Where are those 3000 messages coming from?

Tune It Out

Most people think advertising doesn't affect them — that they can tune it out. You may be thinking that right now. But the goal of advertising is to create an impossible-to-ignore idea. You might think you're successfully tuning out advertising because you don't look at an ad and then run out to buy what it's selling.

But brand recognition doesn't happen with one viewing. When you were a baby, someone probably tried to feed you certain foods over and over and *over* until you accepted the new flavor and texture. Advertising works in the same way. If you see 3000 advertisements a day, you may not realize how many times you're getting the same message.

So, no — you don't scroll through your phone, see a clever ad for shoes and immediately order a pair (well ... maybe sometimes). But just like you're doing with your personal brand, ads are attempting to create an "impression." These impressions can leave an imprint on our minds. (See "Impressions" on page 16.)

We don't *think* ads affect us — but they do. So what's happening?

Come along for the Ride

Picture for a minute that you're floating on a lazy river ride, completely relaxed. The sun is out and ... *splash!* A fake coconut drops from a plastic tree right next to your inner tube. "So irritating," you think. You keep floating and open your eyes. An iridescent bubble floats along next to you. "*Oooh!*" you think. You want to reach out and touch it, but it's so pretty, and you don't want it to burst.

The coconut is one kind of advertising. *Splash!* It attempts to wake you up, hit you between the eyes: *Buy this! Click here! Call now!*

But the bubble is another kind of ad. It looks pretty and doesn't disturb your peace. It might show up on your phone, in your social media, in your comic book — just a gentle message. You might even appreciate what it's promoting.

Let's return to your answers from the beginning: *Is* there a brand attached to what you're wearing, eating, listening to? For most of us, the answer is yes. The most successful campaigns don't even have to point out that they hooked you. They just let *you* do their advertising for them.

Keep reading to learn some of the techniques and tools of advertising, and come to realize how we're all part of advertising's cycle. Think of a magician performing magic. Magic shows are fun to watch because they're entertaining, but also because magicians want us to believe that something is true and possible, even when it seems *im*possible. Do some ads use certain types of illusions for the exact same reason?

Chapter TWO

An AD-venture into Promotion

Marketing 101

The terms *advertising* and *marketing* are sometimes used interchangeably, but they're not the same.

Advertising is the business of drawing your attention to a product or service, and the promotion of that product or service.

Your **2** favorite words are back together ...

BAKE

SALE

This Friday, bring money and find joy.
Cupcakes!
Squares!
Cookies!

Marketing is the business of what, how and where to sell things. Advertising is a part of marketing.

Creating a poster is a popular advertising technique. All the information found on the poster is marketing.

This class represents **Marketing 101**. Each student you see here is playing a role in the marketing cycle. It's like one big group project.

1 **Strategy (aka Planning)** figures out how the brand should be perceived and what methods would be best for reaching the target audience.

STEP RIGHT UP!

2 **Market Research** is the information collector. It can be info from surveys, **focus groups**, interviews, online data — anything that helps pinpoint the customer.

3 **Market Analysis** determines how the product is different from its competition. With market research, the analysts figure out what the price should be.

4 **Art and Copy** refers to the "creatives" — the copywriters and designers who find clever ways to promote the product. Copywriters write the copy, or the text, of an ad (see Chapter Three), and designers create the look. The creatives try to tell a story. Good stories invite us to share in an experience — they make us curious. Designers often use **storyboards** to develop their vision.

5 **Sales** takes everything from the other people in Marketing 101 and reaches out to customers to sell the product.

13

Badger Power

Once a product or service hits the market, advertisers want to build brand loyalty. Brand loyalty is a pattern of repeat buying that stores love. Point systems, reward programs, incentives ... all of these are used to build brand loyalty. This can take years and a whole lot of money. You might think, "But I'm just a kid! I don't have any money! My parents buy everything. What does it matter how advertising affects me?"

Ah, so humble. In the eyes of advertisers, you have HUGE power. Some companies think of all that badgering as **pester power** or the **nag factor**.

According to market researchers, you influence *many* consumer decisions in your family, such as where to
- eat meals (a meal deal ad for families),
- shop for clothes (a back-to-school ad),
- buy devices (cell phone family plan) and
- vacation (an ad for a family-based resort).

Pester power even influences store shelving, which is like in-store supermarket *super* marketing. (Notice the wordplay? Advertisers *love* wordplay!) There are four levels of shelving:
- stretch level — smaller brands that can't afford premium shelf space
- adult's eye level — bestselling brands and higher-priced items
- child's eye level — brands marketers want you to grab
- stoop level — store-brand and bulky items

It's no coincidence that you're face-to-face with characters on cereal boxes (see "Direct and Averted Gaze" on page 40) or that candy, sugary cereals and chips are easy to reach. If you see it, you can pester for it!

Also, brand loyalty can last a lifetime. The products our families use when we're kids are often the same ones we turn to as adults — another reason advertising with kids in mind is so effective.

STRETCH LEVEL

ADULT'S EYE LEVEL

CHILD'S EYE LEVEL

STOOP LEVEL

Culture

Culture is a pattern of behaviors shared by a group of people. This pattern of behavior can be related to the food you eat, the language you speak, the clothing you wear, the music you listen to, the way you celebrate … everything!

Popular culture (aka pop culture) is ever-changing and depends on where and when you live. It refers to the specific activities and products that are aimed at a large part of the population.

Advertising helps to both create *and* reflect parts of pop culture. For a long time, this meant showing a "standard idea" of beauty or family or love. In recent times, ads have begun to reflect the changing nature of all these things with more diverse images, people, ideas and experiences.

You are likely part of more than one culture. For example, each classroom has its own culture. So does each family and each sports team. And each new classmate and new teammate can change a culture.

Belonging to different cultures means we often learn the same information in different ways. But the one thing all cultures share is how people learn through emotion. Feeling joyful teaches you something: *I can coast on my bicycle!* So does fear: *I can fall off my bicycle and hurt myself — I won't try that spin again!*

What happens if advertisers connect a feeling you can relate to with a product?

That ad used an inside joke — and I got it!

The sad images and music in that commercial make me want to donate my money.

That politician said the other candidate lied and hates the environment and wastes all our money.

Impressions

Once an ad has successfully targeted your emotions, it can make an impression. And if you buy what it's selling, it has *definitely* made an impression. This can lead to years of brand loyalty.

AGES 4–5

At this age, children watch TV shows and commercials with equally fixed attention.

⬇

Favorite characters are often used on products to trigger pester power.

⬇

Toys, snack foods, fast foods and family vacations are promoted often.

AGES 6–7

Many children this age do not understand that the purpose of ads is to get them to buy things.

⬇

Since they're still very trusting of what they see, kids tend to believe ad messages.

⬇

Sugared products are heavily promoted.

AGES 8–12

Children this age understand that something is being promoted, but they are still open to persuasion.

⬇

A sense of independent identity is developing, and ads often use language to appeal to that.

⬇

Ads geared to preteens highlight adolescence. Many encourage preteens to buy into a teen culture, so there's a new focus on music and sporting equipment.

AGES 13–19

Teens understand that they're being targeted, but they may not know how often and how well it works.

⬇

This is the time when distance from parents and acceptance by peers are used more and more in ads.

⬇

Ad campaigns tend to focus on either the negative or positive. The negative might be an ad that highlights a teen's insecurities. The positive might appeal to a teen's newfound independence, activism and, ironically, their ability to reject brands.

What impressions have already been made on me?

When It Rains, It POURS

When you were a baby and being fed that same thing over and over, someone probably put a bib on you. When you play certain sports, you have to wear a helmet. And when it rains, you might remember an umbrella. These are all part of the same idea: safeguarding, big and small. When we're aware of what's out there, it means we can make decisions about what we want and don't want.

BUY THIS!

CLICK HERE!

CALL NOW!

ON SALE!

Awareness also means we can take an active approach. So let's turn the tables. Instead of looking at advertising from a consumer's perspective, let's take a look from an advertiser's point of view.

On the following spread are two business ideas: one is a product, and one is a service. We're going to create an advertising plan for each of them by using the techniques and tools that will be revealed in the rest of this book.

THE PRODUCT:

The strategy team shares information in a brief, which is a document that outlines the client's main goals.

The creative team then develops ideas for the campaign.

Bubblarious!®* Bubble Gum

It looks like regular bubble gum but when you blow a big enough bubble it changes color. Each pack is different! You may start with green gum that turns pink. Or purple gum that turns yellow.

Background	Patented new bubble gum technology means only bubbles bigger than a grapefruit create new colors. With the addition of elasticeno™, creating this bubble is challenging but possible.
Goal	Make **Bubblarious!®** a market leader by promoting a candy innovation. Bubble gum was invented in 1928 and hasn't changed much since then.
Target audience	• Kids aged 8–12 with spending money • Market research shows us that grandparents should be targeted due to their interest in (1) buying their grandchildren candy, and (2) sharing in the experience of seeing their grandchildren get a new bubble color.
Focus	We're better than regular gum. *"Bubblarious! Fun with flying colors."* We want a campaign that suggests fun, color and success.
Why buy this?	Tasty and fun, plus a challenge — only 22 percent of our kid testers could change their bubble's color.
Help for the creative team	Social media challenge: Share photos of yourself blowing every bubble color with #bubblarious and win a case of Bubblarious!
Schedule	The client is *wildly* demanding, so have everything ready in the next 24 hours.

Pop!

FUN!

Are you wondering what the ® next to Bubblarious! means? Or the ™ next to Scrap Heap Fleet?

® (registered trademark)

A trademarked product or service that is registered with the government is legally protected around the world.

Your birth certificate is your ®!

THE SERVICE:

Scrap Heap Fleet™*: E-waste Recycling Service

Got e-waste like broken cell phones, laptops and old batteries? Call our fleet of kids on bikes to pick it up and deliver it to our recycling center. You get rid of your e-waste, local kids get jobs and no waste is created in the process. The recycle cycle!

Background	This service is a bicycle-powered fleet of pairs of kids who pick up e-waste for safe recycling. Bikes will be equipped with a cart.
Goal	· Protect the environment by promoting e-waste recycling without creating more waste. · Work locally so kids don't bike farther than a certain radius.
Target audience	Community members who support safe recycling AND youth exercise
Focus	We pick up the electronics cluttering up your space, reduce e-waste and get fit, too!
Why use this?	Everyone has outdated electronics sitting around. Plus, people like to support young workers.
Help for the creative team	For ads targeting parents: Working for SHF means kids are recycling electronics instead of sitting around using them!
Schedule	It's cool — the client's pretty relaxed. (All that biking …)

*These aren't actual trademarked names. They are just made-up names for use in this book.

TM (trademark)

You can use the trademark symbol to identify and distinguish your product from other similar products. Words, logos, names, symbols, shapes and characters can all be trademarked.

Your fingerprint is your trademark.

© (copyright)

You have created an original work and now have the right to, literally, copy it: copyright. You can perform, reproduce or publish it, and no one else can without permission. Copyright laws protect literary, dramatic, musical, artistic and other intellectual works.

You can't copyright an idea. You can only copyright the production of an idea, like a movie, song or book.

Chapter THREE

Map This AD-venture

Maps are used to help navigate journeys. Let's use our own ad map here to do the same. You'll find the following features in all kinds of advertising — including print, online, TV and radio ads — in different combinations.

Claim

This tells you what the product or service will do for you:

> **Bubblarious! We promise it will make you smile.**

Sometimes, a negative claim will be used instead of a positive one to make the advertised item seem like a savior:

> **Stop your e-waste trash cycle. Save the planet with Scrap Heap Fleet today.**

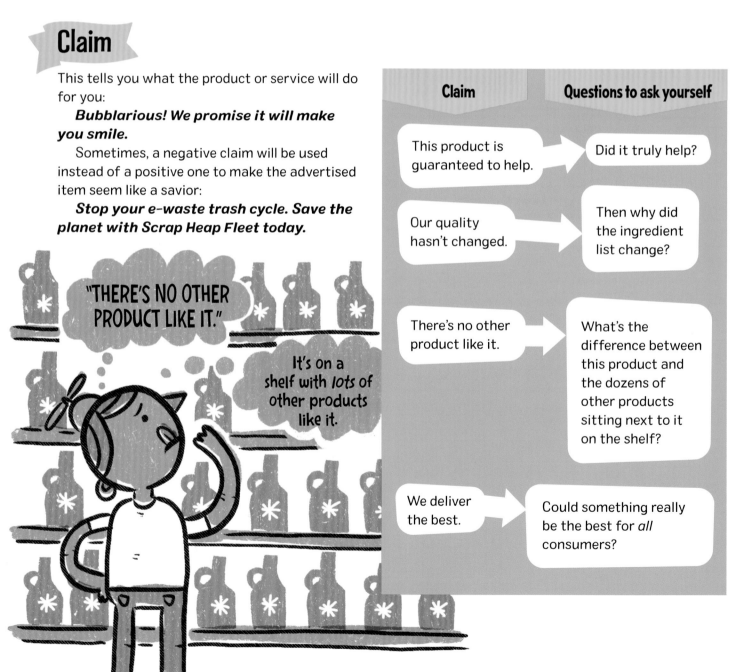

"THERE'S NO OTHER PRODUCT LIKE IT."

It's on a shelf with *lots* of other products like it.

Claim	Questions to ask yourself
This product is guaranteed to help.	Did it truly help?
Our quality hasn't changed.	Then why did the ingredient list change?
There's no other product like it.	What's the difference between this product and the dozens of other products sitting next to it on the shelf?
We deliver the best.	Could something really be the best for *all* consumers?

False Advertising

A claim occasionally uses information that might seem misleading:

Kids who chew Bubblarious! are happier and more popular.

How can they know if those gum chewers are happier? And how are they measuring popularity? The good news is that there are **watchdog agencies** that investigate claims to ensure standards are met and truth is upheld — just like when your teacher fact-checks your work. Some brands and ad agencies even have in-house counsel, or lawyers, working for them, to make sure the claims are factual.

Photo retouching is another element of false advertising. A photograph might be altered to remove lines, pimples, crooked teeth — you know, the things that make us human. When you look at a close-up of a person's face in a magazine and don't see any pores, you may wonder, "Don't I need pores?" (You do.) "Before" and "after" photos can be purposely misleading, too. "Go from *this* to *THIS*!"

Grocery ads can feature terms that sometimes need further explanation, too …

"Healthy" — Healthy *how* exactly?

"Natural" — Wait. The packaging lists **processed ingredients**!

"Pure" — Pure *what*?

Or it can claim something like "cholesterol free!" or "low fat!" when that product never had cholesterol or fat in it to begin with. That would be like you boasting about something obvious, like "I use my nose to smell"!

Slogan

This is the short, catchy phrase in the ad. It's not boastful, like a claim, but it supports the ideas behind the claim. Sometimes a slogan rhymes to increase the chances that you'll remember it.

SCRAP HEAP FLEET

YOU JUST CAN'T BEAT SCRAP HEAP FLEET!

BUBBLARIOUS!

FUN with FLYING COLORS

Tagline

While a slogan is used for a single product or part of an advertising campaign, a tagline is used to represent the company and doesn't change:

Give Scrap Heap Fleet Your E-Waste: We'll CRUSH It!

If your product is unexpectedly popular with a new group — say teens are suddenly buying it — you may want to update your brand with a new slogan, but the tagline will stay the same. Sometimes companies switch the slogan from appealing to parents to targeting kids instead. A tagline is like your last name, and the slogan is your nickname.

SCRAP HEAP FLEET

WE'LL CRUSH IT!

SCRAP HEAP FLEET

Copy

This is the main text in the ad — it supports the claim with more information. In a radio or TV ad, it's the script that's read out loud. Because it's a short message, it is really important to choose the right words in copy.

"You" is used a lot, with the intention of drawing you in and making you feel like there's a connection between the ad and ... well, you.

"Guarantee" is also popular. It's one of those words that make a product seem better than its competition.

"Promise" is a better word to use for kids than "guarantee" — it means the same thing but suggests something a friend might say to you.

"New," "best" and "unique" are other commonly used words — again, to help your product stand out.

Copy often uses comparative language, even when the comparison isn't clear:

Scrap Heap Fleet works with greater efficiency!

Greater than what? OR

Bubblarious! has a better flavor!

Better than what?

In print ads, the copy is displayed in a special font. **Typography**, the art and design of letters and text, helps to convey the message. Think of all the fonts you can use for an assignment. Designers will even create new fonts so that the copy looks right for the brand.

BUBBLARIOUS!

Association

Have you ever looked at an ad and thought, "What do puppies have to do with buying a new bicycle?" Then the slogan makes the connection for you:

Imagine harnessing all the energy of a new puppy into a 10-speed bike!

Do you have an optimistic friend who is so positive and upbeat that people think you're the same just because you hang out together? Or the reverse — a friend who people think may be a "bad influence"? That's the power of association.

The human brain works like this: if you're shown random objects together, your brain will make a connection between them. You might not even be aware that you are doing it. Since so many people like puppies (or ice cream, beaches, kittens, sunshine — you get the idea), advertisers sometimes try to cram them into their ads, even when it makes no sense at all.

OFFER EXPIRES SOON!

Call to Action

This is the bossy part of the ad.

Buy this! Vote now! Don't miss out!

Some might as well use a ticking bomb sound as accompaniment:

LIMITED TIME ONLY!

ORDER IN THE NEXT TWO MINUTES AND RECEIVE A FREE GIFT!

Focal Point

The focal point is about how the composition of the ad draws you in to look at something specific. To understand it more fully, let's look at a key artistic rule created by ancient Greek mathematicians.

If you draw a line inside the main rectangle to make a perfect square (blue), the space left over is another rectangle with the same proportions as the main shape. If you make another perfect square (red), you can see that another rectangle forms. This pattern is called the **golden ratio**. It creates unity and proportion in images.

The yellow line is there to draw your eye to the spiral shape that forms — this becomes the focal point and where the product is often featured. The spiral can appear in different corners of the rectangle depending on the design. Spirals and symmetry are appealing to the human eye.

Special Ingredient

In order to support a claim, advertisers might include a special ingredient in their ads. Did you notice one in the Bubblarious! brief, where it mentioned the addition of *elasticeno*™? (Elasticeno is not real, but it sounds scientific, right?)

Maybe you've seen an ad like this. That elasticeno is special, indeed. Maybe even magic ...

It's a gray day in the skate park.

A child standing alone pops in a piece of Bubblarious!

The bubble suddenly changes color.

Now, the kid is surrounded by other smiling, laughing kids.

The park itself changes to a full-color wonderland of multicolored bubbles. We hear the voiceover. "With the power of elasticeno, the bubble changes color. Bubblarious! We promise it will make you smile."

Testimonial

In advertising, a testimonial is when someone makes an official statement about a good or a service. People don't make testimonials for free. It's typically a paid transaction, meaning they're compensated in some way. Testimonial advertising works in a few different ways:

A An endorsement is when a person publicly gives their support to someone or something. These are often delivered by someone famous because famous people already have the trust and adoration of their fans.

Organizations can also offer endorsements:

The Bubble Champions of North America (BCNA)* proudly endorses Bubblarious!

*Not a real organization (which is really too bad!).

Bubblarious! is the best training ever to be a bubble champ!

B An expert opinion is another kind of testimonial. For example, advertisers LOVE to use doctors. Doctors weigh in to give the product or service legitimacy:

Dr. Fictus guarantees Bubblarious! will make your face strong, or your money back.

But seriously, who's going to return *gum*? The manufacturer knows this, so it's a safe promise. Also, has the Bubblarious! team *really* performed facial strength tests on people?!

C A satisfied customer is a regular person whose life was changed by using this product or service:

"Hold on, listeners — it's another satisfied customer on the line. It's Tom, from Denver! Tell us, Tom — why did you switch from Brand X to the reliable Scrap Heap Fleet service?"

The idea here is that experts or celebrities are not the only ones who will benefit from this product. It's for everyone!

D There are also brand ambassadors and influencers. These people officially represent brands in person and online: everything they publicly wear, say, do and post should be a promotion of that brand. For example, the Bubblarious! influencer would wear the gum's colors and logo, talk about their own "bubbly" personality and post pictures of Bubblarious! contests with friends.

You might be familiar with "kidfluencers" — kids on social media platforms who have millions of followers and are paid by brands to mention, use and endorse products. They've been hired to "relate" directly to you and your needs and wants.

It's the best ever!!

Small Print

Imagine a friend whispering essential information so quietly you can barely hear it.

"Wait, WHAT? There's a surprise quiz today?"

The small print in ads works the same way. Also known as the "fine print," it refers to the tiny words at the bottom of an ad that give you details about the product or offer. Sometimes these hard-to-see messages contain vital information.

For radio and TV ads, a speed reader might deliver the small print, making it hard to understand.

*Chewing Bubblarious! in direct sunlight may result in a permanently stained tongue.

Logo

A logo is a symbol or design that a company uses to identify its product. The logo is meant to identify, inform and attract.

That's a lot to pack into a small space. But many recognizable logos work so well that we don't even realize how much information we're taking in all at once. These logos become part of the visual landscape of our society. Think of professional sports teams, who have some of the best logos out there. A team logo helps to connect you with other fans, making you part of that team's culture.

The idea of **pictograph** symbols has been around since the earliest recorded time. Ancient Egyptians, for example, used a hieroglyphic alphabet to identify, inform and attract. Some logos are just the product name in a special font.

During the **industrial revolution** (1760–1840), businesses started to supply areas outside their own, and they wanted a recognizable product. They literally used hot irons to brand symbols on their wagons, ships and barrels so that merchants would know what was in there. Advertisers used these branded symbols to promote the goods. This is why we call them *brands* today.

How many logos do you see in your backpack? On your phone, granola bar wrapper, yogurt cup, running shoes, binder, sweatshirt … the backpack itself?!

29

Ad Map for Bubblarious!

For a fun product like this, you want bright visuals that pop. *Pop* — get it? This print ad could be used for magazines and comic books.

Slogan

Logo

Claim

Focal point

Call to action

Small print

Ad Map for Scrap Heap Fleet

If you've done your market research for this service, you know that a recent study said 46 percent of public transportation users don't have access to a car. Hello, target audience! These are the same people who may have difficulty getting rid of their heavier e-waste.

Values-based marketing is an attempt to appeal to your ethics and beliefs. For example, maybe public transportation passengers don't have a car because they're actively seeking an environmentally friendly alternative. This would align them with SHF's goals. Also, since passengers will be standing and waiting, these ads can have more copy than ads used in other places. People will have time to read them.

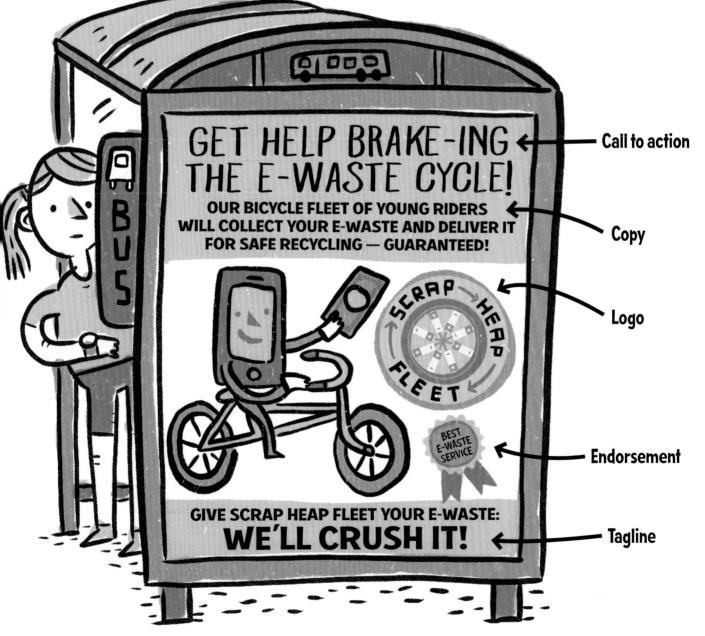

Call to action

Copy

Logo

Endorsement

Tagline

GET HELP BRAKE-ING THE E-WASTE CYCLE!

OUR BICYCLE FLEET OF YOUNG RIDERS WILL COLLECT YOUR E-WASTE AND DELIVER IT FOR SAFE RECYCLING — GUARANTEED!

SCRAP HEAP FLEET

BEST E-WASTE SERVICE

GIVE SCRAP HEAP FLEET YOUR E-WASTE: WE'LL CRUSH IT!

Chapter FOUR

An AD-venture into Your Brain on Ads

Your brain actually changes its shape every time you learn something new. (There! It literally just happened!) You are constantly taking in new information and asking your brain to process, filter and store it. The brain is a three-pound wonder.

These three different areas of the brain perform very different functions:

Reptilian: Takes care of primal needs like eating, drinking and avoiding danger. Also controls your instincts and subconscious. When you feel a tingle down your spine, it's coming from your reptilian brain.

Limbic: "Head" quarters (see what I did there?) for your emotions. Where your memories are created and stored.

Neocortex: The spot for perception and reasoning. (When your reptilian brain sends that tingle down your spine, the neocortex is where it's analyzed.)

Neocortex
rational or
thinking brain

Limbic
emotional or
feeling brain

Reptilian
breathing,
heartbeat and
other automatic
functions

Have you heard your teachers talk about **media literacy**? Well, part of media literacy is being able to understand and critically evaluate the messages sent through different types of media. For this, you need to use your neocortex. That's how you decode all the advertisements coming at you from different sources. If you analyze those ads using your neocortex, you might make better buying decisions.

Many advertisers, though, aren't so interested in your analysis. You might decide not to buy something if you think it through! How can these advertisers tap into your primal and emotional needs (the reptilian and limbic parts of the brain) — and avoid analysis from the neocortex? There are lots of ways. Read on!

Psychological Pricing

This is the theory that certain prices have a bigger psychological impact on buyers than others, making the price seem more reasonable.

▸ **99 Cents:** Since you read from left to right, it makes sense to end a price in 99. This way, $2.99 seems *much* cheaper than $3.00. (At least that's what we tell ourselves.)

▸ **Buy One, Get One Free:** Why get one thing when you can get two? All of a sudden, we're digging through piles of clothing to buy something we don't necessarily need. Thanks, emotion!

Bait and Switch

You see an advertised price for something online. You try to order it, and the seller says, "That item's sold out. What about this [more expensive] item instead?" You buy it.

Wait. Was that original advertised item ever available?

Repetition

Have you noticed how advertisers repeat an ad over and over and *over*?
They replay TV commercials, they display ads across all advertising media —
including print, online and TV — and they restate the slogan in the ad itself.
(Is this why copy is called *copy*?!)

They even duplicate the product in a patterned ad sequence, like the one below.

Thomas Smith, the author of the book *Successful Advertising*, has a good
explanation for why repetition can work:

1st Look

2nd

3rd

4th

5th

You look at an ad. but you don't see it.

You don't notice it.

You're aware that it's there.

You recall seeing it before.

You read it.

10th You ask a friend if they've tried it.

9th You wonder if there's something to it.

8th You roll your eyes and think. "Here's that ad again."

7th You're irritated by it.

6th You reject it.

11th You wonder how much it costs.

12th You're curious if it's any good.

13th You think it might have some value.

14th You think you've wanted this for some time.

15th You want it but can't afford it.

YOU BUY IT!

You carefully count your money.

You're frustrated at your lack of funds.

You plan to buy it.

You accept that one day it will be yours.

20th

19th

18th

17th

16th

This is a lot of repetition to describe repetition. And this explanation has stood the test of time — Smith published his book in 1888!

Repetition can enhance representation. Featuring individuals from different races, ages, genders, sexual orientations, abilities and socioeconomic realities over and over in ads can increase the visibility of marginalized communities. In this way, repetition in ads can serve as an agent of positive change.

Humor

Who's the funniest person in your class? Funny attracts attention, which is the main goal of advertising. But not everyone finds the same things funny. Humor is considered culturally specific, which means what's funny to you might not be for your neighbor.

Charles Darwin referred to humor as a "tickling of the mind," which makes sense because we remember funny jokes (and possibly funny ads):

Q. What did Bubblarious! say to your dog?
A. I'm stuck on you.

Fear

In that reptilian brain, everyone is afraid of something. Advertisers know this and many use it to their advantage. Some ads create both the fear *and* the sense of security that buying the product will provide:

Fear ⟶ **Resolution**

Do I smell bad? If I can smell other people, does that mean they can smell me?

Fear ⟶ **Resolution**

My smile makes me feel self-conscious. I don't have perfect teeth. I'm going to cover my mouth every time I smile or laugh.

Fear ⟶ **Resolution**

How come everyone knows how to dress cool? I don't know how to put outfits together. It makes me not want to hang out with people.

Fear ⟶ **Resolution**

I want to upgrade my phone but I'm afraid that if I throw out my old phone, it'll just contribute to toxic material in the ground and what are we doing to the world?

Fear is a very successful motivator in ads. Fear-based feelings like insecurity, anxiety, guilt, worry and stress can all create impressions that make us want to buy that *one thing* to fix our sensitivities. But where would we be without our sensitivities?

Trust

Trust is usually something that builds over time, but advertisers would love to stop you in your tracks *immediately*. The fastest way to an immediate **hook**? A "trustworthy" face.

We judge a face for trustworthiness through the limbic system — emotion central — and we do it in only 33 milliseconds. (A blink takes about 100 milliseconds, which means we judge a face for trustworthiness faster than we blink!) What facial features are considered trustworthy? Which ones do advertisers want in their ads?

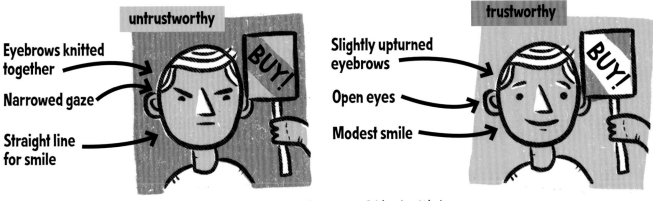

Why does your limbic brain make these snap judgements? Maybe it's because the faces that are deemed trustworthy appear more open and ready to listen. Is that why the people you see in advertisements often seem to look the same?

Sensory Branding

Appealing to your five senses — sound, smell, sight, taste and touch — helps advertisers connect with your emotions. Picture walking through a mall or busy city street during the holidays. Those window displays often feature products with moving parts, flashing colors and repeated music, and even pump out the smell of baked goods! None of this is accidental. Why advertise with just one sense when you can combine them?

This multisensory approach works in print ads, too, with specific copy language that creates links, like this:

Sound

A jingle is a short song or tune intended to sell a product. You might be thinking of a popular jingle right now — that's their lingering power. They first became popular with radio and TV ads, but the roots of jingles go much deeper. In England during the 16th century, street singers were employed by local businesses — like the butcher, baker and grocer — to sing memorable little songs about their products to passersby. One is still sung today: "Hot Cross Buns."

Today, jingles are sometimes referred to as "sonic logos" because they're little, like a logo — usually just a few notes long — and are also instantly connected to the brand.

Like a jingle, the start-up sound your computer makes and the text chime of your phone are trademarked sounds that help create a **sonic brand** to heighten your awareness. Like music, a sonic brand is understood across languages and cultures.

Music is used in 75 percent of TV ads. This is because music helps to create an emotional connection. Have you ever noticed that food commercials are often louder than the show you're watching? This is to increase the stopping power of an ad — to stop you in your tracks to pay attention. Research shows that

- loud music stimulates appetites.
- classical music makes you think you're getting a quality product.
- slow music encourages you to spend more money.
- high-energy music increases brand recognition.

Brands also use music for its ability to stimulate **nostalgia**. Popular music from different eras is used to connect listeners to an earlier time. Scrap Heap Fleet, for example, might use 1950s music in a commercial to make grandparents nostalgic for their youth. To them, the music might imply responsibility and simplicity. It also might remind them of a time when people were less wasteful. They feel like they can trust Scrap Heap Fleet to get the job done quickly and efficiently! Happier emotions = positive association with that brand.

Smell

You're sitting at a bus stop and someone pulls out a bag of popcorn. Instantly, you imagine being at the movies. What just happened?

The inside of your nose detected a smell. The olfactory bulb is the link between nose and brain — it sends messages from your nasal cavity to parts of the limbic system. The limbic system decides if that smell is gratifying (popcorn!) or threatening (eww!). In an impressive filing system, humans can remember 10 000 distinct smells.

We know the limbic system houses memories and emotions, and we know that smell has a direct route to those parts of our brains. Think of perfume and cologne ads — they are selling ambition, captivation, elegance ... not just a fragrance. Many brands have developed their own scent with a combination of smells like vanilla, forest, floral or citrus. Imagine you are in a retail store and you recognize a particular scent. It could become one of those 10 000 smells filed away. Now you're on the bus, and someone in front of you blows a bubble with Bubblarious! You smell its signature smell, which acts like a logo. All you can think about is how much you want some gum ...

Sight

Direct and Averted Gaze: Studies show that a direct gaze sets up an emotional connection.

    Compare this ——

    With this ——

    Which one makes you feel a connection? The direct gaze is used in ads to draw you in.

    Advertisers have also successfully used the averted gaze in one key way: if the eyes in the ad are looking at the featured product, that's another tool for directing where you look.

RED
Energy, like blood. Also **love**, like hearts. Or **alarm**, like traffic signs. It depends on what you're selling and how you use it.

ORANGE
Vitality, like citrus fruit. Also **safety**, like traffic cones.

YELLOW
Warmth and **light**, like the sun. Also, **optimism**.

GREEN
Calm, like forest green, or **energy**, like lime green. **Stability**, like the earth.

WHITE
Clean style.

Color: Color is how your eye perceives the reflected light around you. Colors can provoke emotions, and as you know by now, the main goal of advertising is to connect your feelings to a brand.

    Q. How many color variations can the human eye detect?

    A. Seven million.

    But since we don't have time to review all seven million, let's examine ten.

BLUE
Peace, like the sky and water. **Trust** and **authority**, like banks and police officers. Also, **personal reflection**.

BLACK
Mystery and **seriousness**. The **unknown**, like being in the dark.

BROWN
Reliability and **stability**, like the ground you walk on.

PINK
Sweetness, like candy, as well as **hope** and **caring**.

PURPLE
Luxury, like royalty (popular with expensive beauty products).

Picture some popular logos. Now check their color meanings. Are those logos sending that message?

Q. How quickly do we judge a product?
A. Within 90 seconds.

Q. How much of that judgment is based on color?
A. 60–70%!

Colors have specific cultural meanings as well. The color associations listed on page 40 are common in Western cultures. Since colors have different meanings for religious, spiritual and historical reasons, advertisers change their strategies between countries.

RED: In some Eastern cultures, it means luck and prosperity, but in some African cultures, it signifies mourning.

GREEN: In some Eastern cultures, it signifies birth and new beginnings. In South America, it is said to convey both nature and death.

BLUE: In the Middle East, it's used to convey protection, and in Mexico, it can be used for grieving.

Using green in the package to show its energy sounds like fun. But green is considered a spiritual color in China, and using it for something frivolous like bubble gum could be viewed as insulting. So, for the Chinese market, it would be better to advertise and package the gum in only pink. (The same idea applies for copy — writers are aware that words have different meanings between cultures.)

Taste

Advertisers have a complex job when it comes to taste. They want you to

- try the product.
- like the taste.
- be convinced it's a better-tasting item than its competition.
- buy it regularly.
- share it with people.

Different strategies are used in ads to achieve these goals.

1. They might highlight the product's exclusive flavor and appeal to your adventurous side: *Try the unique taste!* Or the claim might suggest a health benefit that comes with the taste: *Give your morning more tasty energy!*

2. They use terms like *blind-taste-test winner* or *better ingredients* or *new and improved flavor!*

3. They feature the word *delicious* and show happy groups of people enjoying it. Ads want you to feel like a tastemaker: the one who discovered the product and is responsible for its success.

Some advertisers have gone a step further and created actual edible billboards made of *real food*. Imagine huge signs made of cheese, cake, soda, salad, chocolate and fruit. Hmm. What might a Bubblarious! edible billboard look like?

Touch

Imagine touching your phone screen and feeling ... a Bubblarious! wrapper? *Haptic* means an interaction with touch (like braille). The vibration feature on your mobile device is an example of "haptic technology." It creates friction, which communicates a sense of texture on the screen.

This texture can mimic fabric, a candy wrapper — anything! Brands have trademarked sounds and colors — maybe they could also trademark a specific texture.

Touch can also be used to invite you closer, like the direct gaze. Have you noticed that laptops and appliances are left partially open in ads? And phones in stores are left on? This is in-store advertising, and the thinking is that if you get a feel for it, you just might buy it.

In magazines, the ads are sometimes printed on different paper stock. Like the stopping power of the commercial that's louder than the show, the glossy paper might grab your attention. This is also why some junk mail advertising is on high-quality paper — to mimic an invitation that you need to open. A shampoo bottle might resemble the outline of a body, which might convey a sense of vitality. This quality would then be reinforced in a TV commercial.

Even though we can order just about anything online, in-person retail shopping still exists. Why? Mostly, it's because customers like the **tactile** experience of touching clothes, furniture and other products. Touch is an important part of how we live (and buy).

The techniques described in this chapter are used to focus your attention on the product. According to **neuromarketing** tests, 95 percent of the time, our buying decisions go through the reptilian and limbic brains — and never make it to the lonely neocortex. Hopefully, after reading this book, you'll be able to fully activate that neocortex and make more thoughtful and analytical choices.

Chapter FIVE

An AD-venture Tracker

Which of the following activities is tracked by marketers?

- a) visiting a website
- b) tagging a photo
- c) commenting on a friend's post
- d) "liking" something online
- e) starting a shopping cart
- f) breathing

Okay, technically not f, but the rest of them — *yes*! Everything you do is trackable. Some people refer to it as your digital footprint. Like a footprint left in the mud, your digital footprint is a trace of your actions online. Your digital footprint creates a path directly to marketers, who follow and interpret your data.

Imagine a detective following you around, making notes and dusting for fingerprints:

Suspect: Age 11

7:32 a.m. — Ate a bowl of cereal. Left bowl in sink.

7:56 a.m. — May or may not have washed hands.

7:58 a.m. — Refused to wear coat. Shivered outside.

8:04 a.m. — Ate granola bar en route to school.

8:48 a.m. — Borrowed pencil from classmate.

What could advertisers promote with this information? Cereal, hand sanitizer, adaptable clothing for indoor/outdoor temperatures, packaged snacks, a pencil case ... And this is all before 9:00 a.m.!

Now imagine what advertisers could do with all the digital footprints you leave online ...

Your Digital Footprint

Advertisers are interested in three key pieces of information: *who* you are, *where* you are and *when* you're online. They can collect all of this information from data they retrieve from the digital footprints you've already shared.

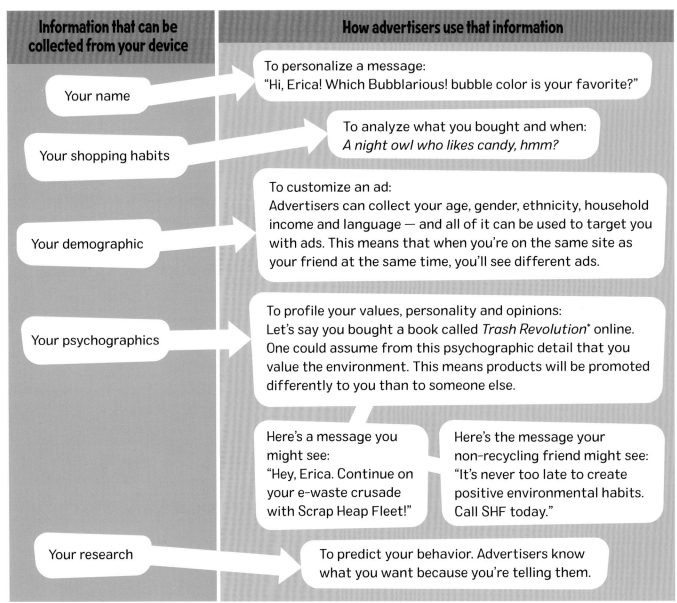

Information that can be collected from your device	How advertisers use that information
Your name	To personalize a message: "Hi, Erica! Which Bubblarious! bubble color is your favorite?"
Your shopping habits	To analyze what you bought and when: *A night owl who likes candy, hmm?*
Your demographic	To customize an ad: Advertisers can collect your age, gender, ethnicity, household income and language — and all of it can be used to target you with ads. This means that when you're on the same site as your friend at the same time, you'll see different ads.
Your psychographics	To profile your values, personality and opinions: Let's say you bought a book called *Trash Revolution** online. One could assume from this psychographic detail that you value the environment. This means products will be promoted differently to you than to someone else. Here's a message you might see: "Hey, Erica. Continue on your e-waste crusade with Scrap Heap Fleet!" Here's the message your non-recycling friend might see: "It's never too late to create positive environmental habits. Call SHF today."
Your research	To predict your behavior. Advertisers know what you want because you're telling them.

*A real book! That I wrote! (See what I did there?)

Here's how it happens:

You begin a search online, or visit a website, or download an app on your phone. Small text files called **cookies** are implanted in your device and saved on your hard drive. You are now being tracked.

Data companies collect the data and sell it to advertisers. Before you know it, you've been targeted.

Also, those security updates you ignore? They protect your device when a bug is identified. A bug can make your safe device insecure, sending your data who knows where.

Private Eye

You might be thinking, "Great! I get ads delivered to me for things I already want to buy. What's the problem?"

Why *do* we care about privacy?

Let's look at it this way: the activities tracked by marketers are stored in a search history. This history reveals your private interests, likes, dislikes and fears. Do you really want to share that with everyone? Since you don't control where your data goes, it might show up as ads that interest you. It might also be used to promote something you're against, either to you or to someone else.

We're asked to give up our right to privacy every time we want to access a site or app. In this way, our privacy starts to lose its meaning. Imagine what would happen to society if we were asked to repeatedly give up any other of our human rights. The internet *seems* to be free, but we pay for it with our privacy.

Each new generation changes the idea of what privacy should mean. In 1840, when the first postcard was sent, many people were shocked. Letters that weren't sealed in an envelope that *anyone* could read — WHAT?!

Your path of digital footprints is tracked through ...

Your Apps

When you download an app, it's like putting a tracking feature in your mobile device. Advertisers now know how you live in the virtual *and* physical world. This means they know what you do, where you are, what you buy and who you know.

In-app ads are so seamless, we don't always realize we're being targeted. Advertisers like in-app ads because they share demographic and geo-location data — in other words, who and where you are. Let's say you have the Bubblarious! app on your phone. We can find you and send you a Bubblarious! ad based on your location:

Get ready to bubble over with joy! Bubblarious! is sold two minutes away at the Candy Mart.

Because of the code implanted on the digital ad, the advertiser can now track how many people like and share the ad. If you do like it, the advertiser can then use your name in ads to your friends:

Join Erica in the #bubblariouschallenge!

Have you ever received a birthday message from a company? That's an example of how technology companies work with advertisers to gather detailed info and target you.

Nudging is the practice of quiet and repeated suggestions to make you notice something. The supermarket shelving mentioned in Chapter Two is a kind of nudging. For Scrap Heap Fleet, imagine a series of arrows on the floor leading out of a subway station. The arrows could be matched with a cheeky message:

Stop staring down at your phone and safely recycle that e-waste!

The arrows could lead to a booth outside that explains SHF's service. If you check the SHF website at the station or booth, advertisers can track it, testing the impact those arrow ads have on consumers. The ☞☞☞ gently nudged you exactly where they wanted you to go.

Are you under the age of 13? That means, legally, you shouldn't have your own social media account or have any personal information collected online without a parent or guardian's consent. Many countries have agencies and laws that protect children under the age of 13. In the United States, the Children's Online Privacy Protection Act (COPPA) deals specifically with the security of children's online data. The same is true in Canada with PIPEDA (the Personal Information Protection and Electronic Documents Act), which enforces the law that you have to agree to the collection and use of your personal information. Geolocation data, photographs and videos are all off-limits to collect if you're under 13 and your parent or guardian hasn't given permission.

Your Social Media

The most popular social media apps for kids and teens are photo and video messaging apps.

The "feed" on social media is the stream of content you scroll through. An in-feed ad is placed between the content on your feed, or before or after it begins or ends. Since the ad often looks like your other content, you might take in the information without even registering that you're looking at an ad. Remember the bubble from Chapter One — the one that doesn't disturb your lazy river ride? That's the goal of in-feed ads.

If you click on an in-feed ad, it looks like this:

In-feed ads are an example of native ads, and they don't only appear on social media. Even legitimate news sites have them, sometimes in the form of a surprising headline that makes you want to click on the article. Native ads also look like search listings, promoted listings and **advertorials**.

Native *video* ads are also popular. How-to videos, sketches, skits and advergames are everywhere. Advergames are games created to showcase a product — the game itself is just one giant commercial!

Speaking of ...

Your Games

Ads are also placed *inside* existing games. With over two billion gamers worldwide, gaming has blown up (pun intended). Popular ads in games include billboards, political posters and logos in city scenes. Game worlds also showcase **product placements** like foods, drinks and cars.

Your playing patterns — what game you play, when you play it and who you play it with online — produce data, which is then used to create more targeted ads in games.

So. Many. Footprints.

Right now it's a one-way trail — you leave digital footprints and other people analyze them. But … what if your personal data was treated like a valuable resource from which YOU could benefit?

"Data dignity" means being able to decide where your data goes and who gets to use it. The future model envisioned by some computer scientists is a two-way system: you continue to leave digital footprints, but you're compensated if someone wants to use them. Your data is the gas that runs the advertising machine! Why let others fill up for free?

Chapter SIX

A Time Travel AD-venture

How did we get here, you ask? This constant promotion, the knowledge of how to access our wants and fears? Let's take a little trip through time …

6th or 5th century BCE: The first coins are stamped with images of conquerors to spread pride throughout regions, an early example of **propaganda**.

1448

Invention of the printing press. Books are made, and there's leftover paper for print ads.

1835: The first known billboards are printed.

1930s–40s

Moms interviewed say that radio ads are very effective at getting their kids to beg for items.

1935: Market research begins, giving advertisers insight into what the public wants and how they should sell it.

1950s

The first TV remote control is invented. Advertisers need new strategies to keep audiences from changing the channel. Plus, Saturday morning cartoons begin airing! Kids start watching hours of ads.

1953: TV shows for preschoolers air — and so do their targeted ads.

Timeline: 1800 | 1900 | 1910 | 1920 | 1930 | 1940 | 1950

1874: British parliament passes legislation to protect kids from merchants targeting them.

1926

The first radio jingle plays.

1920s: Loyalty clubs for children's products begin.

1946: The first **focus group** is conducted.

1945: A **baby boom** creates a bigger ad audience for cars and appliances.

1941

The first TV ad airs (before a baseball game).

1894

The first **brand mascot** is introduced at the Lyon Exhibition in France.

1913

The first **movie trailer** is shown.

1900: Advertisers use product placements in children's stories.

1955: Academics begin studying children's buying habits. The same year, advertising agencies hire psychologists to help understand consumer thinking.

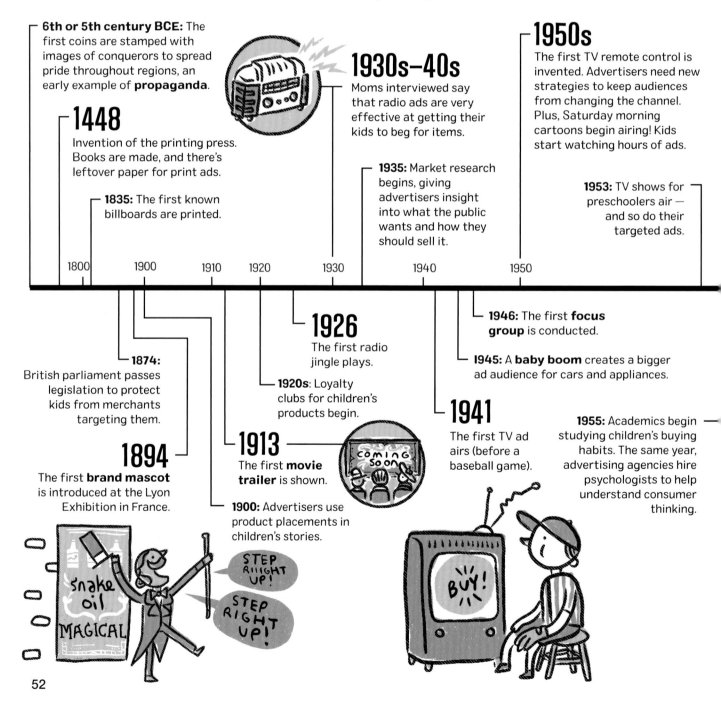

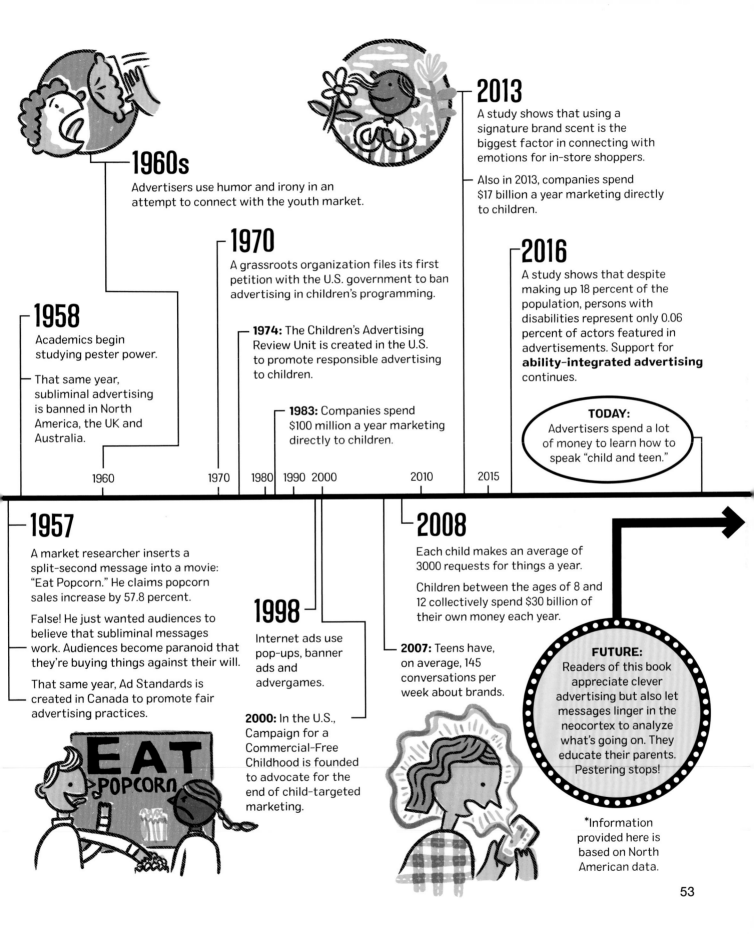

1960s
Advertisers use humor and irony in an attempt to connect with the youth market.

2013
A study shows that using a signature brand scent is the biggest factor in connecting with emotions for in-store shoppers.

Also in 2013, companies spend $17 billion a year marketing directly to children.

1970
A grassroots organization files its first petition with the U.S. government to ban advertising in children's programming.

1974: The Children's Advertising Review Unit is created in the U.S. to promote responsible advertising to children.

2016
A study shows that despite making up 18 percent of the population, persons with disabilities represent only 0.06 percent of actors featured in advertisements. Support for **ability-integrated advertising** continues.

1958
Academics begin studying pester power.

That same year, subliminal advertising is banned in North America, the UK and Australia.

1983: Companies spend $100 million a year marketing directly to children.

TODAY:
Advertisers spend a lot of money to learn how to speak "child and teen."

1960   1970   1980   1990   2000   2010   2015

1957
A market researcher inserts a split-second message into a movie: "Eat Popcorn." He claims popcorn sales increase by 57.8 percent.

False! He just wanted audiences to believe that subliminal messages work. Audiences become paranoid that they're buying things against their will.

That same year, Ad Standards is created in Canada to promote fair advertising practices.

2008
Each child makes an average of 3000 requests for things a year.

Children between the ages of 8 and 12 collectively spend $30 billion of their own money each year.

2007: Teens have, on average, 145 conversations per week about brands.

1998
Internet ads use pop-ups, banner ads and advergames.

2000: In the U.S., Campaign for a Commercial-Free Childhood is founded to advocate for the end of child-targeted marketing.

FUTURE:
Readers of this book appreciate clever advertising but also let messages linger in the neocortex to analyze what's going on. They educate their parents. Pestering stops!

*Information provided here is based on North American data.

EAT POPCORN

Chapter SEVEN

An AD-venture into Your Personal Brand

Marketers use personality questions to increase traffic (and to target you with ads based on your answers). Let's try to crack your personal brand code by applying the techniques described in Chapters Three and Four.

Personality Questions

1 In my class, I'm the best …
A. student. **B**. athlete.
C. artist. **D**. prankster.

2 I've been caught in a lie …
A. only once. (I might be lying.)
B. Lie? ME?
C. a bunch of times, unfortunately.

3 My friends often …
A. become dramatic.
B. expect a lot of me.
C. come up with great ideas.
D. make me smile.

4 On social media, I …
A. edit photos before posting them.
B. notice which photos get the most likes and repeat similar styles.
C. think that posting photos has made me a better photographer.

5 This is the motto I like best:
A. I'm stronger than people know.
B. Life is what you make of it.
C. I want to be the change in the world.

6 Friends would know my favorite candy flavor.
A. Yes **B**. No

Your Personal Brand

A statement like this could be your claim. We often compare ourselves to others with personal claims — about grades, sports, hair color, artistic ability … everything. Advertisers want their products to stand out, and people like to stand out, too.

Do you use false advertising to boost your personal brand? Rare is the person who doesn't occasionally add in misleading information to support their claim!

These are your associations. Is your friend group based on associations that you want to have?

Your photos tell a lot about you. Is there a focal point in your photos that frames what's important to you?

Just like a tagline, a motto is a short phrase that captures your beliefs. It's meant to answer the question "What's most important to you?"

If your friends can name that flavor, they know your taste. Why do you like it?

Personality Questions

7 When I want someone's opinion, I ask …
A. my friends. **B.** my parents.
C. my teacher/coach. **D.** my pet.

8 These are the images I doodle or post a lot:
A. favorite characters
B. favorite team logo
C. my initials

9 I like to hear certain songs on repeat.
A. Yes **B.** No

10 I buy products because they smell good.
A. Yes **B.** No

11 I wear a favorite color a lot.
A. Yes **B.** No

12 My favorite clothes look AND feel a certain way.
A. Yes **B.** No

13 When I'm fearful, I wonder if …
A. I can stop feeling that way.
B. my fears stop me from doing stuff.
C. my fears could be a guide.

14 Certain people always make me laugh.
A. Yes **B.** No

Your Personal Brand

These are the trusted advisors who provide your testimonials. You can ask them for help and encouragement — and you know they will always endorse you.

Your personal logo could be in your doodles. Tattoos and monograms — are they just another kind of logo?

Remember how music — or sound — can create an emotional connection? Your song will get brain-filed away as part of the soundtrack of your life.

You might be crafting your signature smell — shampoo, detergent, lip balm — in ways you hadn't realized.

Does your favorite color send the message you want? Should you strategize color for different events?

Favorite clothing and stuffed animals can provide comfort and security through touch. Touch influences what you buy.

Fear is a powerful emotion. Have you ever bought a product to help quash a fear? Did it work?

If someone makes you laugh, it means they understand your humor — and also your brand personality!

Brand: You!

Has anyone ever told you that you're not acting or sounding like yourself? You might be trying to change your personal brand in a way that surprises people. Perhaps you're presenting a brand that's different than the one most people see.

Cultivating your brand requires these marketing roles.

Strategy:
Who do I want to be friends with, and how do I make it happen? Or, how do I get on my teacher's good side?

Market Research:
I hear a lot of things about other people — it probably does affect my opinions of them.

Market Analysis:
I spend time figuring out how I'm different from my friends.

Advertising Art and Copy:
I never thought of having a brand personality, but I do show different versions of myself to different people. The clothes, scents, hairstyles, makeup and music I choose are no accident.

Sales:
Follow me on social media! Donate to my crowdsourcing campaign! Share my posts and images!

Besides privacy, your brand also trades in social currency — the value of your social connections — both in person and online. The currency is exchanged in likes, comments and emojis. Trading in these things helps you understand the perceived value of your brand.

Having a brand — or many brands — means that you understand the complexity of living in the world. Navigating all the different social expectations is like launching your own campaign over and over again.

If you had to define your brand, you might say all of these different things at different times:

CONCLUSION

Let's take a look at your passport to see where we've traveled on this *AD-venture* ...

We launched our own advertising campaigns for Bubblarious! and Scrap Heap Fleet, and we created maps to guide our way. We delved inside our brains to discover how advertising gets into our heads, and learned how our paths are tracked online. We time-traveled through advertising's most significant dates, and we even deciphered our own personal brands.

Every day, you are bombarded with ads trying to tell you what "success" and "normal" look like. But who says you have to accept those ideas? Hopefully, knowing ad tools and techniques will strengthen that neocortex filter, allowing you to question the endless messages. Sometimes a message will speak to you, other times it won't. If a message offends you, contact the brand and let them know.

By learning how advertising works, you can think more critically about ads and decide which ones align with your beliefs and your view of the world. If you travel to another country where people speak a different language, you do your best to learn how to communicate. You learn the language!

And now you've learned the language of advertising.

Since advertisers have such a useful assortment of tools in their toolbox, you might think this means that advertising is always successful — *guaranteed*!

Not true! Consumers are human, after all, with individual tastes and wants. Even though the ability to target you is becoming more and more refined, the power you have to choose what you really want is the most fun part of being a consumer. If you bought everything advertised to you, you'd be in debt AND trapped under a heavy pile. All that stuff would just slow you down. Insert spokesperson voice here: *Mad for Ads* is perfect for AD-venturers everywhere. (Ooh, that's a good tagline. We should ™ it.)

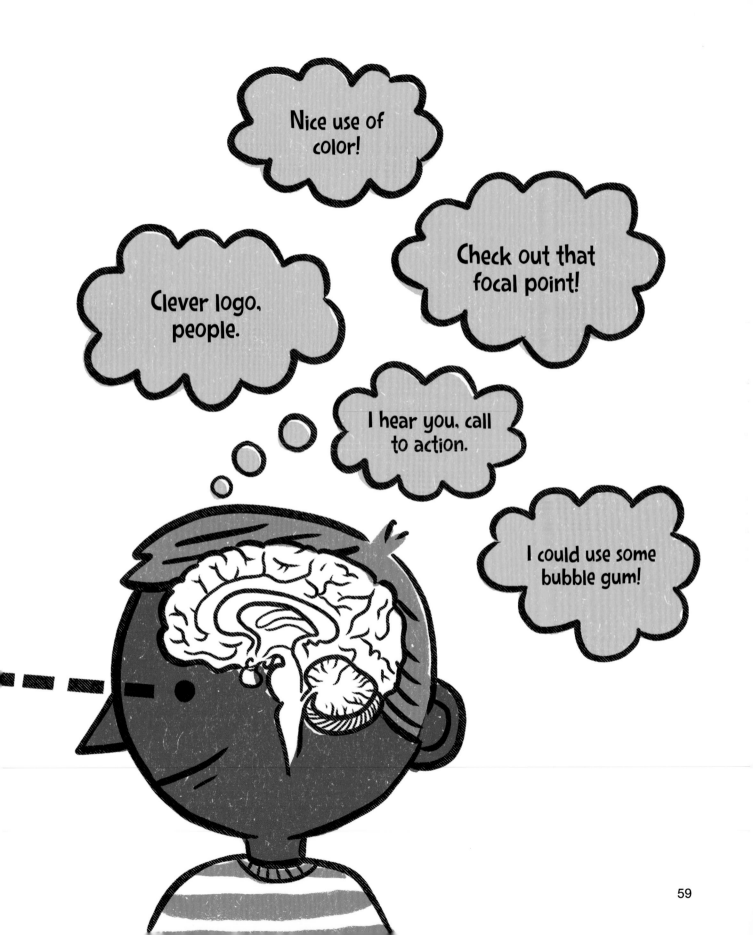

Glossary

ability-integrated advertising: when individuals with disabilities are included in advertisements, specifically for products and services intended for all people

advertorial: an advertisement that gives information about a product or service in an article format

baby boom: a significant rise in the birth rate, such as in the U.S. following the end of World War II

brand mascot: an animal or character that represents a brand

cookie: a tiny data message sent from a website and saved on your web browser. The next time you visit the website, your browser sends the cookie to the server, allowing it to customize information sent back to you.

focus group: a small group of people who are studied by researchers to determine their response to something. Today, advertisers use focus groups to test new flavors, logos, ideas — you name it. The idea is that the small focus group will represent the response from a larger group. It is an example of the user becoming part of the design and creation process.

golden ratio: a number calculated when the long part of a line segment is divided by the short part, and this equals the entire length of the line divided by the long part. The golden ratio is found in art, architecture and nature, where it creates proportion that is pleasing to the human eye.

hook: something used to capture your attention and encourage you to buy. In the great sea of media, you are a fish that advertisers are hoping to hook with a short phrase or jingle.

industrial revolution: a time period of major changes in how products were made, due to new technology and the use of machines, that lasted from roughly 1760 to 1840 in Europe and North America

media literacy: the ability to identify different kinds of media (books, TV, movies, games, newspapers, etc.) and understand their messages

movie trailer: in 1912–13, an advertising manager for a movie theater company realized the benefits of showing ads between movies to a captive audience. They began making trailers, or movie ads, in which upcoming attractions would play at the end of the feature. (Even though they play before the movie now, we still call them trailers.) Today, movie trailers are some of the most shared content pieces on social media.

neuromarketing: the use of brain science to understand how advertising and marketing affect consumers. Your brain gets hooked up to a machine where your responses to products, designs and campaigns can be measured by brain activity.

nostalgia: a longing, wistful feeling for the past

pester power or **nag factor:** the ability for children to get adults to buy them things by begging and pleading over and over

pictograph: an illustrated symbol for a word or phrase

processed ingredients: the ingredients in foods that have been altered during their preparation. Not all processed foods are unhealthy, but the ones that add fat, sugar and salt usually get our attention as "junk food."

product placement: when a specific product or brand is shown in the background, used by a character or spoken about in a movie or TV show you're watching or a game you're playing

propaganda: the spreading of ideas or information to influence public opinion and beliefs. It differs from advertising because it doesn't attempt to encourage sales of a product or service.

representation: the portrayal of something or someone. When we ask for diversity in advertising, it means we're asking for greater images of all walks of life.

sonic brand: the overall strategic use of sounds and music to support a brand

storyboard: a series of illustrations used to show a proposed design sequence

tactile: able to be perceived by touch

target audience: in advertising, the specific group at which the ad campaign is aimed (e.g., kids, teens, parents, cat owners, hockey players, bubble gum fans, etc.)

typography: the art and technique of designing and arranging the letters and symbols in printed matter

watchdog agency: a person or organization that stops illegal behavior. Watchdog agencies for advertising protect consumers by investigating claims.

Bibliography

Articles

Clark, Hugh M. *et al.* "Who Rides Public Transportation." American Public Transportation Association (January 2017).

Committee on Communications. "Children, Adolescents, and Advertising." *Pediatrics* 118, no.6 (December 2006): 2563–69.

Neal, David T., and Wendy Wood. "Childhood Advertising and the Unconscious Mind." *Psychology Today* (March 2014).

Rupp, Rebecca. "Surviving the Sneaky Psychology of Supermarkets." *National Geographic* (June 2015).

Wilcox, Brian. *et al.* "Report of the APA Task Force on Advertising and Children." American Psychological Association (February 2004).

Websites

adage.com
changingminds.org
colormatters.com
consumerwatchdog.org
mediasmarts.ca

Radio

CBC Radio. "Is Handing Over Personal Data the 'Price of Admission' to Modern Life?" *The Sunday Edition*, March 1, 2019. cbc.ca/radio/thesundayedition/the-sunday-edition-for-march-3-2019-1.5038795/is-handing-over-personal-data-the-price-of-admission-to-modern-life-1.5039128

CBC Radio. *Under the Influence*. Hosted by Terry O'Reilly. cbc.ca/radio/undertheinfluence

Books

Brophy Down, Susan. *Power and Persuasion in Media and Advertising*. New York: Crabtree Publishing, 2018.

Curtis, Andrea, and Peggy Collins. *Eat This! How Fast Food Marketing Gets You to Buy Junk (and How to Fight Back)*. Markham, ON: Red Deer Press, 2018.

Dooley, Roger. *Brainfluence: 100 Ways to Persuade and Convince Consumers with Neuromarketing*. Hoboken, NJ: Wiley, 2011.

Kidd, Chip. *Go: A Kidd's Guide to Graphic Design*. New York: Workman Publishing, 2013.

Lanier, Jaron. *Who Owns the Future?* New York: Simon & Schuster, 2014.

Levitin, David J. *This Is Your Brain on Music: The Science of a Human Obsession*. New York: Dutton, 2007.

Lupton, Ellen. *Design Is Storytelling*. New York: Cooper Hewitt, 2017.

Ogilvy, David. *Ogilvy on Advertising*. New York: Vintage Books, 1985.

Smith, Thomas, and J. H. Osborne. *Successful Advertising: Its Secrets Explained*. Smith's Press, 1888.

Index

ability-integrated advertising, 53, 60
advertising goals, 10, 18, 19, 36, 40, 50
advertising history, 29, 35, 38, 52–53
advertising techniques, 11, 12, 16, 17–19, 34–43
advertorials, 50, 60
apps, 47, 48, 50
art, 13, 23, 56. *See also* design
associations (connections), 23, 24, 29, 38, 42, 53
    color, 40–41, 55
attention, 12, 16, 36, 38, 43, 48–49, 60
averted gaze, 40
awareness, 10, 17, 24, 29, 35, 38, 50

behavior, 6, 15, 46, 48, 50
belonging and acceptance, 15, 16
billboards, 42, 50, 52
brains, 24, 32, 36, 39, 43, 60. *See also* limbic brain; neocortex; reptilian brain
brand, 6, 12, 29
    ambassadors, 27
    connection to, 38, 40
    loyalty, 14, 16, 52
    mascot, 52, 60
    personal, 6, 54–57
    personality, 8, 55, 56
    recognition, 10, 38
buying
    decisions, 14, 33, 43, 58
    habits, 52
    power, 14, 58

call to action, 24, 30
characters, 14, 16
children
    advertising to, 14, 16, 18, 22, 52, 53
    protecting, 49, 52, 53
Children's Online Privacy Protection Act (COPPA), 49
claims, 20, 21, 23, 26, 30, 42, 54
clothes, 6, 14
colors, 37, 40–41, 55
comfort, 36, 55
commercials, 16, 35, 43
compensation, 27, 51
competition, 13, 20, 23, 42
consumers, 5, 13, 58, 60
    protecting, 53, 61
copy, 13, 23, 31, 41, 56
copyright, 19
copywriters, 13, 41

critical thinking, 33, 58
culture, 15, 29, 36, 38, 41

data, 6, 44, 46–47
    analysis, 6, 46, 50, 51
    children's, 49
    collection, 46, 49
    online, 6, 13, 49, 51
    personal, 46–51
    selling and sharing, 46, 48, 51
    tracking, 44, 46–49
    See also information
decisions, 5, 17, 43, 51, 56, 58
demographic, 46, 48
design, 23, 25, 29, 60. *See also* art
designers, 13, 23
devices, 14, 38, 43, 46
digital footprint, 44, 46, 48, 50. *See also* data
direct gaze, 40
disabilities, people with, 5, 53
diversity, 5, 15, 35, 53, 60

emotional connections, 38, 40, 55
emotions, 4, 15, 16, 32, 34–40, 42
    anger, 15
    anxiety, 36
    connecting with, 15, 37, 42, 53
    fear, 15, 36, 55
    guilt, 15, 36
    joy, 15
endorsements, 27, 31. *See also* testimonials
expert opinions, 27

faces, 37
false advertising, 21, 54
famous people, 27
fine print, 28, 29
focal point, 25, 30, 54
focus groups, 13, 52, 60
followers, 6, 27
font, 23, 29
food, 14
    advertising, 14, 16, 21, 38, 42
    processed ingredients, 60

gaming, 50
gaze, 40
grandparents, 18, 38
guarantee, 20, 23
guilt, 15, 36

haptic technology, 43
headlines, 31, 50
history, advertising in, 29, 38, 47, 60
hook, 37, 60
humor, 36, 53, 55

impressions, 10, 16, 36
influencers, 27
information, 12, 13, 28, 32, 46. *See also* data
ingredients, 26, 60
insecurities, 16, 36
internet, 47
    ads, 48, 50, 53
    bug, 46
    cookies, 46
    search history, 47
    traffic, 54

jingles, 38, 52, 60
judgments, making, 37, 41

language, 16, 23, 37, 58. *See also* words, use in ads
laws, 19, 49, 52
lawyers, 21
learning, 15, 32
limbic brain, 32, 33, 37, 39, 43. *See also* brains
logos, 8, 29, 30, 31, 39, 41, 55
    placement of, 28, 50
    sonic, 38

magazines, 30, 43
market
    analysis, 13, 56
    research, 13, 18, 31, 52, 53, 56
    target, 41
marketing, 12, 56
media literacy, 33, 60
misleading information, 21, 54
movie trailers, 52, 60
music, 37, 38

nag factor, 14, 60. *See also* pester power
native ads, 50
neocortex, 32, 33, 43, 53. *See also* brains
neuromarketing, 43, 60
news sites, 50
nostalgia, 38, 60
nudging, 48–49

online activities, 44, 46–50.
    See also data

packaging, 41, 43
paper, 43, 52
parents, 4, 14, 19, 22, 49, 52
Personal Information Protection
    and Electronic Documents Act
    (PIPEDA), 49
personality, 6, 54, 57. *See also*
    self, sense of
pester power, 14, 16, 53, 60.
    See also nag factor
photographs, 6, 21, 54
pictographs, 29, 60
popular culture, 15
postcards, 47
posters, 12, 50
prices, 13, 34
print ads, 23, 30, 37, 43, 52
privacy, 47, 56
product placement, 50, 52, 61
products, 8, 12–13, 14, 17, 18, 27, 29, 38
promise, 23
propaganda, 52, 61
psychographics, 46
psychology, 34, 49, 52

radio ads, 23, 27, 38, 52
reading, 31, 34
repeat buying, 14
repetition, 10, 25, 35, 48
representation, 5, 35, 53, 60
reptilian brain, 32, 33, 36, 43.
    See also brains
rule of thirds, 25. *See also* design

sales, 13, 56
satisfied customers, 27
schedules, 18, 19
self, sense of, 4, 6, 16, 31, 54.
    See also personality
senses, 37
    sight, 37, 40
    smell, 37, 39, 53, 55
    sound, 37–38, 55
    taste, 37, 42, 53
    touch, 37, 43, 55
services, 12, 17, 19, 27
slogans, 22, 24, 29
small print, 27, 29
Smith, Thomas, 35
social media
    activities, 6, 54, 56, 60
    ads on, 18, 50
    children and, 27, 49, 50

sonic brands, 38
stopping power, 37, 38, 43
stores
    advertising in, 43, 53
    shelving in, 14, 20
storyboards, 13, 61
strategies, 41, 42, 52, 55, 56
strategy team, 18
subliminal messages, 53

tactile, 43, 61
taglines, 22, 31, 54
target audience, 6, 12, 18, 19, 31, 52, 61
targeted ads, 46, 48, 50, 54
teens, 16, 19, 50, 53
testimonials, 27, 55. *See also*
    endorsements
text. *See* copy
textures, 43
trademarks, 18–19, 38, 43
trust, 16, 27, 37, 38, 55
TV ads, 23, 28, 35, 38, 43, 52
typography, 23, 29, 61

watchdog agencies, 21, 61
window displays, 37
words, use in ads, 21, 23, 37, 41, 42.
    See also language

Promotional consideration provided by...

Helen Antoniades, Krista Black, Alexandrea Brooks, Christine Hibbard, Gill Goldsmith, Tristen Gottlieb Sturm, Gillian Gunn, Maureen Hall, Kate Hemblen, Karen Jordan, Kingston WritersFest, Nikole Kritikos, Danielle Lamothe, Tim Lewis, Wayne Lilley, Patrick Lohier, Lori Lucier, Penny McDonald, Leah McTiernan, Steve Miller, Amelia Munro, Mary Partridge, Julie Payne, Molly Peacock, Julie Schmidt, the Design Museum (London), the Museum of Brands (London), the International Literacy Association, the Toronto Public Library, Colleen Tillotson, Jennifer VanderBurgh, Jan Vogtle and Maryanne Ware.

Kristie Painting and Jennifer Usdan McBride, my industry experts who read an early draft and gave detailed, helpful notes.

Yvette Ghione, Naseem Hrab, Olga Kidisevic, Yasemin Uçar and everyone at Kids Can Press.

Barb Kelly and Ian Turner, for making it look so good.

Lisa Lyons Johnston, president and publisher at Kids Can Press, for ensuring a balanced approach in the writing to properly reflect an industry that means a great deal to her. Your notes were essential.

Also, Jennifer Stokes, who wrote after reading my initial proposal, "Erica, this is very exciting!!!" and maintained that level of enthusiasm and kindness for over two years. I'm very grateful for your guidance and your friendship.

Copyeditor Catherine Dorton and proofreader Doeun Kwon for your careful review.

Kathleen Keenan, for your patient and helpful collaboration right from the beginning.

Loretta Fyvie, Peter Fyvie and Nicole Fyvie for being my loyal champions.

Marzipan and Clover for being such good company while I wrote.

And, finally, to Jay, Liv and Grace Lilley, for everything, always.